"Many in the field talk about financial lit[e] financial empowerment. What a gift to t[.]

—TIM RANZETTA, CO-FOUNDER, NEXT GEN PERSONAL FINANCE

"As our younger generations leave college with more debt than ever before, they're also leaving without the financial education needed to handle it. The results have been disastrous. In *The Missing Second Semester,* Gene gives us a view into what can be done about that problem, and just a few others that have an outsized influence on how well our financial lives can unfold. He also shows us why he is one of the most concise and clever financial educators working today. *The Missing Second Semester* is a must-read, and a must-give to anyone looking to start their financial lives on the right foot."

—JOE TORSELLA, PENNSYLVANIA STATE TREASURER

"*The Missing Second Semester* is another home run for Gene! He offers practical, common-sense ideas regarding personal money management in an easy-to-understand way. Bravo!"

—DANIEL N. HEBERT, DIRECTOR OF PROFESSIONAL DEVELOPMENT, JUMP$TART COALITION

"*The Missing Second Semester* is a powerful weapon in the righteous fight for financial independence. Targeted toward young adults, it delivers practical insights for all of us on being smarter with our money."

—BRIAN PORTNOY, CFA, FOUNDER, SHAPING WEALTH

"*The Missing Second Semester* fills an important educational gap, presenting a comprehensive, but easy to follow, introduction to investing. As the second book in the Missing Semester series, this title makes an important contribution to financial education helping to address the critical need for financial literacy for the younger demographic—who will benefit most from the read."

—DR. GREG FILBECK, CFA, DIRECTOR, BLACK SCHOOL OF BUSINESS

— THE —
MISSING
SECOND SEMESTER

— THE —
MISSING
SECOND SEMESTER

GENE NATALI

foreword by Tim Ranzetta

The Missing Second Semester

HARRIMAN HOUSE LTD
3 Viceroy Court
Bedford Road
Petersfield
Hampshire
GU32 3LJ
GREAT BRITAIN
Tel: +44 (0)1730 233870

Email: enquiries@harriman-house.com
Website: harriman.house

This edition published in 2022 by Harriman House
Copyright © 2020 The Missing Semester, LLC

The right of The Missing Semester, LLC to be identified as the Author has been asserted in
accordance with the Copyright, Design and Patents Act 1988.

Paperback ISBN: 978-0-85719-982-9
eBook ISBN: 978-0-85719-983-6

British Library Cataloguing in Publication Data
A CIP catalogue record for this book can be obtained from the British Library.

Cover design by Brian Taylor
Interior book design and layout by Hunt Smith Design

The Missing Second Semester is dedicated to the students brave enough to ask questions. Because the unasked question goes unanswered.

TABLE OF CONTENTS

Foreword
i

Author's note
YOUR AGE IS AN
OPPORTUNITY
III

Chapter 1
AVOIDING THE QUICKSAND
1

Chapter 2
PLANTING A SEED
5

Chapter 3
PREPARING FOR WINTER
9

Chapter 4
THE POWER OF KNOWLEDGE
17

Chapter 5
UNDERSTANDING
OPPORTUNITY COST
21

Chapter 6
WHAT IT MEANS TO INVEST
25

Chapter 7
THINKING AHEAD
33

Chapter 8
THE STOCK MARKET AND
THE S&P 500
39

Chapter 9
RULES OF INVESTING
45

Chapter 10
PREPARING FOR THE WORST
51

Chapter 11
THE DIVIDEND REWARD
57

Chapter 12
WHEN NOT TO INVEST
63

Chapter 13
PUTTING IT ALL TOGETHER
69

The Bottom Line
WHY MONEY MATTERS
75

FOREWORD

Tim Ranzetta
Co-founder, Next Gen Personal Finance

Fewer than one in five high school students crossing the graduation stage have taken a course in personal finance. (Montana State University research, 2020)

The mountain of outstanding student loan debt now exceeds $1.6 trillion. Most Americans lack emergency savings. Fewer than a third of millennials invest in the stock market. The depressing statistics seem to only worsen with each economic crisis, leaving more people in financial distress. Unfortunately, absent the requisite education in school, the lessons in managing money come mainly from the school of hard knocks. These are the lessons from late fees, high-interest debt, ballooning student loan balances, insufficient savings.

As a co-founder of *Next Gen Personal Finance,* a non-profit committed to financial capability for all students, I partner with an amazing community of 30,000 personal finance educators across the country. These are teachers committed to making a difference in the lives of their students. Yet 80% of high school students are missing out on the essential coursework these teachers offer.

That is why Gene Natali's book, *The Missing Second Semester* is absolutely critical. It closes these educational gaps.

Personal finance teachers repeatedly ask me, "What book can my students read to augment what they are learning in my classroom?"

The Missing Second Semester will now top my recommended list. I first met Gene when he delivered a keynote address at a national conference of financial educators. His passion for the topic was immediately evident, along with his engaging teaching style and his knack for "hooking" the audience with real-life examples to motivate behavioral change. Likewise, his ability to come up with analogies to explain challenging financial concepts— another of his superpowers.

These "hooks" and analogies make *The Missing Second Semester* a must-read. They make personal finance both approachable and engaging.

Here are just a few questions from the book to grab attention and get young people to read further:

· Do you know what four money choices account for 96% of consumer debt?

· Why should every school start a Watching-Trees-Grow Club?

· Would you rather be wealthy or look wealthy?

· How can a cheaper car you buy at the age of 18 be worth almost $400,000?

But it's Gene's common-sense advice on investing that every student should read. His chapter on the cardinal rules of investing breaks down this challenging topic in ways both easy to understand and to act upon. No talk of P/E ratios or how to win a stock market challenge competition. Nope. Just good common sense approaches that all students can implement, starting now.

Dollar-cost averaging becomes, "Buy a little bit, a lot of times." When stock markets correct, as they inevitably do, his book counsels, "When something of value that you want to own goes on sale, buy more."

Even if the vast majority of high school students are missing that semester of personal finance they want and need, all is not lost. *The Missing Second Semester* fills the gaps in a way that is engaging, easy to understand, even inspiring. Many in the field talk about financial literacy; Gene's book is a roadmap to financial empowerment. What a gift to the next generation!

YOUR AGE IS
AN OPPORTUNITY
WILL YOU CHOOSE WISELY?

In an EMERGENCY we are taught to *Call 911.* Dial that number and trained professionals respond. Right? We expect firefighters, paramedics and police officers to arrive on scene with the proper equipment and training. They are responsible for lives. We expect surgeons, auto mechanics, teachers, airline pilots and others to be similarly prepared. But what if they weren't?

What if they were never taught the essential skills?

Their actions would have consequences.

The first *Missing Semester* book, a financial guide for young adults, was intended to help readers understand that their money choices have consequences, and that they're in charge. That book has since been incorporated into high school and college courses across the nation. While the title pointed to the widespread absence of education about money in most schools, the idea for the book came from recognition of the sheer number of people living paycheck to paycheck. These are people in the "real world" who had completed their education, held good jobs, and who in most cases, were making enough money. On paper they had done everything right.

The pieces didn't add up. What happened, and why?

It turns out, they simply weren't taught this subject—*financial literacy.* Many of these people living paycheck to paycheck had made one or two money mistakes, often when they were young, and frequently because they didn't know better.

Our financial choices have consequences. So understanding those choices is vital.

Each year hundreds of thousands of high school students (and their parents) take out student loans. The documents they sign require, under law, repayment of those loans.

How many of these families are being taught what that means—and how to repay those loans?

Each year hundreds of thousands of college students get their first credit card.

How many are being taught the consequences of not repaying the whole loan balance each month?

Each year millions of young Americans starting their first job are handed enrollment forms for their company retirement plan.

How many are being taught how to begin investing the money in that plan?

Money is one of the few subjects that affect every American, and there remain lessons to be learned.

Financial literacy, a basic understanding of how money works, is only the first lesson.

Financial empowerment, in which people gain the ability to take action, is the critical second lesson. It is the primary focus of this book.

To start, **consider your age an opportunity, powerful enough to transform your life.**

CHAPTER 1
AVOIDING THE QUICKSAND

On January 1, 2020, we (you, I, and everyone else in America) woke up owing 14.15 trillion dollars. That's the money that we, as individuals, are legally obligated to repay, the sum of all Americans' personal debts.

Here are the components.

Mortgage (house) debt	$9.86 trillion
Student-loan debt	$1.51 trillion
Auto-loan debt	$1.33 trillion
Credit-card debt	$0.93 trillion
Other debts	$0.52 trillion
TOTAL	**$14.15 TRILLION**

SOURCE: FEDERAL RESERVE BANK OF NEW YORK[1]

Buying a house, paying for college, buying a car, and not paying off the credit card bill are expensive debt decisions. Decisions that result in many Americans paying today's bills with tomorrow's paycheck.

These four money choices account for a staggering **96% of personal debt in America.**

What if, instead of falling behind on these four debts, you think differently, and use each expense decision as *a chance to get ahead?* For example,

Attend a college or school that costs you slightly less than you can afford—then *save and invest the difference.*

Buy a first car that costs slightly less than another possibility—then *save and invest the difference.*

Pay off your credit card in full each month—and *never* suffer the high-interest penalty on any money you don't repay immediately.

Rent a first apartment (or later, buy a first house) that costs slightly less than your price limit—then *save and invest the difference.*

Why?

Because interest isn't just something you pay (on a loan). On an investment,

Interest is something you earn.

That is, if you have money to invest. And you likely will if you make these four debt decisions wisely.

Being aware of the consequences of your money choices is a start to successful investing.

CHAPTER 2
PLANTING
A SEED

Speaking of investing, let's talk about trees. What if every high school and college started a new club on campus? Called *The Watching-Trees-Grow Club*.

You'll need a tree, a place to plant it, approval to plant it, and of course, members.

Grab a shovel, and let's get to work!

After you plant the tree, arrange chairs in a circle or semicircle around it. Next, sit down and watch the tree grow. Meet every day as a club, and watch your tree grow.

Pssst, there is a problem. The day after you plant the tree, it looks the same. A year later it looks nearly the same. And during the winter, when the leaves dropped off, it looked even smaller. Hint, there is an investment analogy here . . . .

Your classmates who didn't join the club walk past each day. They can see the tree doesn't look like it's growing. Keeping members is going to be hard . . . , recruiting new members, even harder.

But we know what the eyes can't see. A tree has a strong foundation, its roots, and *they* are growing. The stronger the roots, the taller the tree can grow. Still, your tree isn't generating much excitement, and the club dwindles down to a small, but loyal, group.

Blink.

You receive an invitation in the mail for your (gulp) 20-year reunion. The invitation says, "Meet at the *big tree in the school courtyard.*" When you pull into the parking lot and see the "big tree," you smile. It's the tree you planted. It worked!

Your friends who dropped out of the club likely feel a tinge of regret. When things don't happen instantly, people tend to lose interest. Our tree took 20 years to grow. And now everyone at the reunion wants a tree that looks like the one you planted! So how do we get them to join the club? And to stick with it?

Here's one idea. What if we changed the name of our club from *The Watching-Trees-Grow Club,* to *The Watching-Money-Grow Club?* Better yet, what if *The Watching-Money-Grow Club* worked the same way?

What if a small amount of money grew into something large? In the case of our club, *not* joining might be the biggest money mistake your friends will ever make.

Money does grow the same way—if you invest it wisely.

CHAPTER 3
PREPARING FOR WINTER

Alaska is a beautiful state. Beautiful, with a very long winter. So long, that when it isn't winter, residents must use that time to prepare for next winter. Without enough food, firewood, and other essentials, winter can be more than just cold.

The same can be said about money. Especially when we don't have enough.

As a member of our imagined Watching-Trees-Grow Club, think about helping your "tree" survive a hard winter—and saving you from having to cut it down for firewood. Preparing for problems is the first step. Preventing them is the second.

Here are two important tools to prepare for coming financial winters and prevent the problems they can bring —**insurance** and **emergency reserve fund(s).** Understanding both will protect you and your saving and investing accounts in hard times.

INSURANCE

It's a necessary evil when you don't need it, but critically important when you do. Insurance protects us from events that have a low probability of occurring, but that can have a large financial impact if they do.

While we all need insurance, we do not all need every kind of insurance, nor do we need it at every point in our life. Here is a summary of the basics.

HEALTH INSURANCE

This is a must have. The probability of needing it may be low, but the possibility of high-risk, high-cost events, with catastrophic long-term consequences for your financial well-being, makes it essential. Health insurance is typically covered by employers. It can be an important part of your compensation, although in most cases you still pay a portion of the expense. Ask your employer for all the details.

Cost-saving strategy. You can be included on your parents' or guardians' plan until you reach age 26.[2] Check the cost of this health insurance compared to buying insurance on your own. After 26, explore the options through your employer or your state.

AUTO INSURANCE

Required by all states. As an operator or owner of a motorized vehicle, you assume the risk of driving. This insurance protects you by reimbursing anyone or anything that might be affected by an accident you are responsible for.

Cost-saving strategy. If it costs less, and you are eligible, stay on your parents' or guardian's auto insurance policy. Pay them for your share of the monthly premium and be smart with the money you just saved (more on this soon). It's a win-win scenario.

RENTERS INSURANCE

This insurance reimburses you for the loss of things you own and keep at the room, apartment, or house you are renting—clothes, computers, audio and other equipment, furnishings, valuables, etc. Get a price quote and think about having this protection.

HOMEOWNERS INSURANCE

This is not required until you own a house, but it *is* required then. Homeowners insurance covers not just your house, but everything in it. Don't be under-insured. Think about how much it would cost to replace everything in your home.

LIFE INSURANCE

The good news: life insurance is generally not necessary—until you have a family or someone dependent upon you and your income. But it *is* necessary then. They—your family and/or dependents—receive the life insurance payout, in cash, after you die. There are two types.

Term insurance. Low cost, big benefit. This is insurance in its purest form. For all the reasons mentioned above, you're protecting your dependents—children, spouse, etc., against financial hardship should something happen to you. Term insurance renews each year and should be renewed while you have dependents.

Permanent insurance. This is a continuous form of insurance, as opposed to insurance that is renewed annually. It is more expensive than term insurance but is in effect for your entire lifetime.

Here are a few basic insurance terms to know, all of which apply to the insurance types on the previous page.

Policyholder
An individual who purchases insurance.

Insurance policy
A contract that defines your insurance, listing what specifically is covered. An insurance policy with $10,000 for roof repairs means that the insurance company agrees to reimburse you for up to $10,000 for damage to your roof.

Insurance claim
A formal request by a policyholder to an insurance company for reimbursement in the event of a loss or policy event.

Insurance premium
The amount you pay for your insurance policy per year.

Insurance deductible
The amount of money you are responsible for paying before the insurance policy kicks in. If that insurance policy with $10,000 for roof repairs has a $500 deductible, you will pay $500 'out of pocket' (your pocket) before the insurance policy pays any remaining repair amount, up to $10,000.

Insurance co-pay
A fixed-dollar amount that you pay before receiving the service covered by your insurance policy. A medical co-pay of $25 per doctor visit simply means that regardless of your overall medical insurance coverage, you pay $25 for each visit to the doctor. The co-pay is an expense that is separate from, and in addition to, your deductible and premium.

EMERGENCY RESERVE FUND

This a natural extension of the insurance topic. An emergency reserve fund is for contingencies (unexpected adverse events) not covered by insurance, such as without warning losing your job. Not having a reserve fund can derail an entire investing/saving effort; so you should try to build an emergency fund that includes three to six months of living expenses in a checking or savings account (that is, cash).

To determine how much to keep in reserve, **ask yourself two questions.**

How self-sufficient would you be without a paycheck?

For how long would you be comfortable without one?

While building up your emergency reserve, there is another instrument to include, kind of a secret tool. **Your Roth IRA can and should be considered part of your emergency fund.**

A Roth IRA is a tax-sheltered investment/retirement account that will be explained soon. It's a way to grow your money tax-free and still have it at your fingertips in case of an emergency.

The money you contribute to a Roth IRA can be withdrawn at any time with NO PENALTY, and the money earned by the investments in the account can be withdrawn at any time with a 10% penalty in the form of a tax on your early withdrawal.[3] The hope is that you don't need to touch this money, even in an emergency, but you can sleep easier knowing that it is there. Paired with the cash in your bank account, enough for 3-6 months of expenses, a Roth IRA creates a layer of security in the event of long-term job loss or unexpected emergencies.

Used wisely—with the knowledge you now have—both **insurance** and an **emergency reserve fund** are vital for building your financial freedom.

Note: You should not use your Roth IRA as an emergency fund until after you have exhausted your primary emergency reserve—your checking/saving account (sustaining you for three to six months). *Even then, making a down payment on a home or car is not an emergency. Neither is taking a vacation.* The Roth IRA is an important emergency reserve, but secondary. When you see the earning power of your Roth account, you'll understand why it should be secondary. The opportunity cost of pulling out this money for anything other than a true medical/health/family/job loss emergency is too great.

CHAPTER 4
THE POWER OF KNOWLEDGE

Would you rather *be* wealthy or *look* wealthy? Because the money we spend to appear wealthy typically comes at the expense of actually *being* wealthy. It is difficult to do both. In most instances, these are conflicting goals, competing for the same dollars.

Elon, a high school senior, had saved $1,100 with plans to trade in an old car for a similarly old, but slightly more expensive, truck. He wanted a truck. Before buying, Elon asked his personal finance teacher for advice on whether he was making the right choice.

How many of us would consider alternatives to buying a vehicle that we had already taken for a test drive?

In this case, the teacher later explained that Elon chose not to buy the truck. He had carefully considered his options and instead put $1,000 into a Roth IRA account, investing that money in a large-company stock fund.

The best money choices you make are those you make before you buy your first stock, bond, or mutual fund. Elon demonstrated this lesson. Said differently,

The best investment decisions are those that give you the money to invest.

Suppose Elon only made the one contribution to his Roth IRA, and doesn't invest another nickel for the rest of his life. Any investment has the potential for loss as well as profit, and past performance carries no guarantee of future returns. But if the S&P 500 stock-market index (described in Chapter 8) does what it has done over the past 50 years—that is, returns what amounts to an average of about 10% a year[4] for the whole period—this single decision, to invest $1,000, one time, at age 18, would be worth $142,000 when he is 70.[5]

It's a powerful statement. **A one-time investment of $1,000 would be worth $142,000!** Can you take this same step?

If you do not believe it's possible, you aren't alone. At the University of Pittsburgh, a student of mine emphatically asserted that if it were possible to turn $1,000 into that much money, *everyone in America would be doing it.* Yep. But only if they knew it were possible. And that's the problem.

Think back to our Watching-Trees-Grow Club. It is possible, but only if you **join the club,** and **stick with it.**

Knowledge *is* power.

Your income (no matter how high) will not determine your ability to retire or live as you wish. **It will be your savings and investments.**

Start *now.* Begin by saving just a dollar a day, more if you can. Think of it like this: if you made $10 an hour at work this past summer and worked 8-hour days, you are choosing to invest your earnings from just your first 6 minutes of work .... Imagine what could happen if you invested the money from your first hour of work, a full $10, each day?

How many of your friends, teammates, classmates, and family members don't know how investing works? What could happen if every high school and college student in America knew what Elon learned?

CHAPTER 5
UNDERSTANDING OPPORTUNITY COST

Let's look at one more decision about car buying and investing. There are over a billion cars on the road today; so a lot of people can relate to this money choice.

Michelle graduates from high school in two months and is looking to buy her first car, a used one. She targeted a price range of $10,000 - $13,000 and used a variety of online resources to search for the right car. Finally, she narrows her choice to two cars, coincidentally at the respective edges of her price range. The two vehicles are similar in mileage and quality.

Here's a short, three-question, multiple-choice quiz to help Michelle make her decision.

1. What is the difference in price between a $10,000 car and a $13,000 car for an 18-year-old high school senior?

a) $3,000   b) $4,000   c) $5,000   d) $380,000
The correct answer is $3,000

2. What is the largest possible difference in cost between a $10,000 car and a $13,000 car for an 18-year-old high school senior?

a) $3,000   b) $4,000   c) $5,000   d) $380,000
The correct answer is $380,000

3. If you are a high school senior, would you rather have

a) a $13,000 car?   b) a $10,000 car and $380,000?

Easy, right? The correct answer is . . . well, actually it's your choice; you're in charge.

Confused? When most of us think about the "cost" of a car, we think of these four expenses: insurance; maintenance; fuel; and financing (auto loan). Few of us add the fifth, and biggest cost—*opportunity cost.*

Opportunity cost is what you give up by making the purchase.

In Michelle's case, the opportunity cost could be $380,000 if she buys the $13,000 car. **Here's how we get to that amount.**

Assume Michelle can afford the $13,000 car, but knowingly purchases the $10,000 car. She qualifies for a five-year auto loan with a 5% interest rate. Had Michelle bought the $13,000 car, she would pay $245 per month. By choosing the $10,000 car, she will pay $189 per month and save $56 each month for the five years of the loan.

- The $56 she saves each month is the *difference in cost,* which Michelle then deposits into her Roth IRA investment account. She does this every month for the full five years of the auto loan.

- Michelle invests the money she deposits in her Roth IRA in an S&P 500 stock fund, and the S&P 500 again provides a long-term return of 10% per year (average).[6]

At 70, in this example, Michelle will have saved $380,000 **from a single smart money choice** made at age 18: she bought a $10,000 car and not the $13,000 car that she had figured she could afford.[7]

The math works the same if you are considering a $15,000 car versus an $18,000 car, a $30,000 versus a $33,000 car, or even a $100,000 versus a $103,000 car.

What matters is the difference between what we pay and what we can afford.

What if you can afford a $25,000 car, but buy a $15,000 car and do what Michelle did? Or do you even need to buy a car?

Understanding the *opportunity cost* of your money choices is a major gain in your financial know-how—and likely, your future net worth. This type of decision-making is life changing: knowingly buying something for less than you can afford, and actively investing that money, as Michelle did.

CHAPTER 6
WHAT IT MEANS TO INVEST

Have you ever sat on a bench or on a blanket in the shade of a tree? Lost in thought, you took the tree completely for granted? Likely. Which, by the way, would highly offend the members of our Watching-Trees-Grow Club.

Would you notice if *all* trees were gone and there were no shade? Likely. We have a propensity to take the things we have for granted. A tree has grown and now gives shade because a seed was planted. The seed grew into a tree.

Investing works the same way. You start with something small, care for it, stick with it, and before you know it, have something large.

Investing is as simple as this tree analogy makes it seem. Unfortunately, people often use big words and confusing language when talking about investing. Fear, mistrust and lack of understanding weigh so heavily on people that 45% of Americans do not invest.[8]

This book, *The Missing Second Semester*, is for high school students, college students, and recent graduates. The "how to" of investing is relatively simple at this point in life. Your career is ahead of you and so is most of the money you will make, both working and investing.

Time is your most valuable investment tool.

You'll never have more of it . . . .

In general, we have worked for 42 years before retiring.

This table shows the potential investment earnings for a 22-year-old who just accepted his or her first job and signed up for the company retirement plan, a 401(k) (explained in Chapter 7). The table shows the estimated future dollar amounts earned in the plan at three different possible rates of return.

WHAT MIGHT YOUR CAREER-LONG INVESTMENTS ADD UP TO?

years worked	42
your monthly contribution	$196
employer's monthly "match"	$196
total invested per year	$4,700
total invested over career	$197,000

YOUR RESULTS

ending value from annualized 6% return	$850,000
ending value from annualized 8% return	$1,480,000
ending value from annualized 10% return	$2,650,000

It's a powerful demonstration. But, where did the $4,700 invested each year come from?

Many companies match their employees' contributions to the company retirement plan, most commonly a 401(k) plan. The table assumes a 4.7% company match (U.S. average),[9] for a salary of $50,000 (U.S. average).[10] And the employee contributed **enough (the miniumum necessary) to receive the maximum match.**

"Annualized" is an average. It does not mean a return of 6%, 8%, or 10% every year. Some years the return is more, other years less. Having your career and a lifetime of earning power ahead of you allows you to take "investment risk" at this stage of life. With time on your side, you can invest in stocks rather than in bonds. Financial pros call this investing in "equity," because stock represents an ownership stake in companies. This is what you *should* be investing in for the first two-to-three decades of your career.

Equity investing has the greatest return potential in the long term but the greatest risk of loss in the short term.

Equity investing includes buying individual stocks or, better yet, baskets of many stocks via a mutual fund or exchange-traded fund/ETF (definitions and explanations coming soon). Buying, at the age of 22, 18, or even 16 (any age, really), a fund consisting of many large-company stocks is likely the best investment decision most of us will ever make.

MONEY AND INVESTMENT VEHICLES

Different types of investments come with different risks and different potential returns. Some returns are guaranteed but most are not. Generally, the greater the investment risk, defined as the possibility of losing money, the greater the potential investment return, and vice versa. Here are the basic money and investment vehicles you should be familiar with.

CHECKING ACCOUNT

Great for paying bills and providing for daily wants and needs. Not an investment account but your money is protected and guaranteed by the bank.

SAVING ACCOUNT

Typically pays a small amount of interest. Possible uses include an emergency reserve fund, and protection from overdraft(s) in your checking account. Protected and guaranteed by the bank.

CDs

Certificate of Deposits. Generally, pay a higher interest than checking and saving accounts, but your money is locked up for the length of the CD (3 months, 1 year, 3 years, and so on). If you withdraw early, there is a penalty. Possible uses when you are young include matching with short-term goals. For example (and this is stretching the possibilities), buying a house in 12-24 months, or (really stretching) planning now for next year's spring break trip. This money is protected and guaranteed by the FDIC (a federal government agency) up to $250,000 per bank.[11]

BONDS

These are loans, typically to a company or institution, in return for which you are paid back more than you invested—an example of *interest you can earn*. Riskier than bank accounts and CDs, but generally safe, they pay a slightly higher interest rate. Typically, the longer you loan your money, the higher the interest rate, but the greater the risk. Loans to the U.S. government (such as U.S. Treasury bonds) are explicitly protected and guaranteed. Loans to corporations (corporate bonds) are not.

STOCKS

Ownership stakes in companies, giving stockholders a stake in the companies' future earnings. Stocks offer the opportunity to participate in the growth of a company or an industry. But this investment type is neither protected nor guaranteed, and your entire investment is at risk.

MUTUAL FUNDS

These combine, usually for a small annual fee, individual-company stocks, and/or bonds and other securities into a single investment vehicle for purchase by investors. Because they comprise many companies, and often industries, in a single investment instrument, mutual funds provide more diversification (and so less risk) than individual securities. A good way to invest in a large number of companies.

ETFs (EXCHANGE-TRADED FUNDS)

Like mutual funds, ETFs combine individual stocks, bonds, and securities into a single vehicle carrying a small annual fee (usually slightly lower than the fees for mutual funds), for purchase by investors. ETFs provide more diversification and less risk than individual-company securities and are an excellent way to invest in a large number of companies.

Note: One important difference between ETFs and mutual funds is that ETFs can be bought and sold throughout the day, whereas mutual funds can only be bought or sold once a day, and after stock-market trading has closed for the day.

YOURSELF, THE MOST VALUABLE INVESTMENT YOU CAN MAKE

Do not underestimate yourself, your value today, tomorrow, and many years from now. Investments in education, training, career, health, and time with your family and friends will all have significant benefits.

As you get older, decisions are likely to get more complicated. A good professional financial advisor may be helpful. Until then, focus on gaining the confidence to invest with understanding.

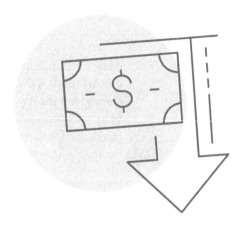

One more thing.

If you choose not to invest, your chance of losing money is 100%.

That's because of inflation, which is the increase in price of the things we buy. The price of your favorite milkshake will be higher years from now when you are enjoying it on a beach in retirement compared to what it will cost you, say, next weekend.

Investing in equities (stocks) is the best hedge against inflation in the long term. The investment return of stock market indices has consistently and meaningfully out-performed inflation over most time periods. This means your money is growing faster than prices of the things you buy. Your spending power is now increasing.

Understanding how to start investing is *the missing piece* in financial literacy education. It is the primary emphasis of the second half of this book.

CHAPTER 7
THINKING AHEAD

For generations people around the world have built their lives on the dream of providing their children, and their children's children, with a better life than they themselves have had. Achieving a dream that big comes with sacrifice.

Still, you might be surprised at how common questions like this are.

"What can I do for my 21-year old son? I'm 55 years old. I never saved, and don't have enough time now. I'll have to work until I die, but I'd do anything for him. What can I do to ensure that he has a different future?"

Time is the critical word here. Being 21 years old with student debt isn't nearly as frightening as being 55 years old with $0 in savings and investments. **Time is the reason.**

If someone in your life is sacrificing the second half of her/his life for your education, can you talk about that choice with that person? And make sure it's the correct choice? You can borrow money to go to college. That person can't borrow money to retire.

And it's time we start talking about 'retirement'—really, financial security later in life—so that you don't have to work until you die, unless you choose to.

RETIREMENT IN AMERICA IS CHANGING

When they retired, your grandparents and maybe even parents may have received a 'pension,' a fixed dollar-amount payment every month, from their former employer—for life—kind of like a salary. The money was guaranteed in return for the number of years they worked for that company. That fixed-payment pension is called a *defined-benefit* plan. And it's on the way out. Sure, it still exists, mostly for those in the military, in government, in fire and police work, in K-12 education, and in many unionized trades.

The organization providing the defined benefit assumes all the investment risk and guarantees that the former employee's pension money will be there. Even better for the employee, if the investment returns do not equal the money owed to retirees, the organization must come up with the difference. But there's the problem. In financially difficult years an organization might not be able to come up with the difference. It then begins a hard-to-win game of catch-up. This can happen to even the biggest and oldest institutions.

If you have a defined-benefit plan, fight for it. It is a powerful retirement vehicle. For everyone else, it's important to know that it likely won't be available in the future. Your future financial security will rest on you. *You're in charge.* The more knowledge you have, the more prepared you will be.

WHAT IT MEANS

Retirement plan options now place the investment risk in the hands of the employee. Let us acknowledge that change is occurring but take a different perspective. Replace the word "risk" with the word "opportunity."

Retirement plans now give employees the investment opportunity.

Yeah, yeah, but they give you the *risk* along with it, of course. Not to worry. With basic investment know-how, you can not only handle it, you can thrive on it.

Common Retirement Plan Options

401(k)

The employee-directed retirement vehicle most commonly offered by companies. Contributions are made with before-tax dollars. This means that your contributions are subtracted from your income before your income taxes are calculated; so contributing lowers your income taxes each year that you contribute. In turn, you will be taxed when you withdraw the money, years from now, after your investment earnings have grown tax free. You may begin withdrawing the money at age 59 ½ and must begin withdrawing at 72.[12]

403(b)

A 401(k)-like retirement plan for employees of non-profit and tax-exempt organizations.

457(b)

A 401(k)-like retirement plan for employees of state and local governments.

IRA

An **Individual Retirement Account.** To contribute, you must have had a job, and you cannot contribute more money in any calendar year than you made that year. As with a 401(k), contributions are made with pre-tax dollars, investment earnings grow tax free, and withdrawals will be taxed.

→

Roth IRA

As with an IRA, you must have earned income and cannot contribute more in any calendar year than you made that year. But here's the important difference from a 'regular' IRA: your contributions to a Roth IRA are not subtracted from your taxable income and do not reduce your income tax in the year you make them, but *withdrawals are tax-free.* This is a huge advantage if you are young and have a low tax rate while you are making contributions. It is especially an advantage if your income tax rates are higher (likely) years from now when you withdraw your funds.[13]

Roth 401(k)

Combines into a single option the benefits of the 401(k) (higher contribution limits) and Roth IRA (your contributions are made with after-tax dollars, while withdrawals are tax-free). This, too, is a great deal for young employees.

WHAT HAPPENS NEXT

After you open a retirement plan, the next step is choosing how to invest the money. There are tens of thousands of investment options, and millions of ways to blend them. Overwhelming, right?

Keep it simple. Your age affords this luxury. Here are two investment options to consider for the first 20 years of your investing career. **An S&P 500 index fund** and **a target-date fund.** The S&P 500 and the important role it plays as an investment deserves its own chapter.

Here's what you need to know about **target-date funds.** They invest your money and then change the mix of those investments automatically as you near retirement, reducing investments with long-term advantages and increasing those with short-term benefits. If that sounds like a pretty good way to simplify those millions of possibilities, go for it. Select a target-date fund for the year you expect to retire and contribute regularly. For example, a 2065 target-date fund is designed for someone looking to retire in 2065. The fund will take investment risk for the first many years, and then slowly shift toward less risky investment types—such as bonds—as retirement, or the time when you'll need the money; gets closer.

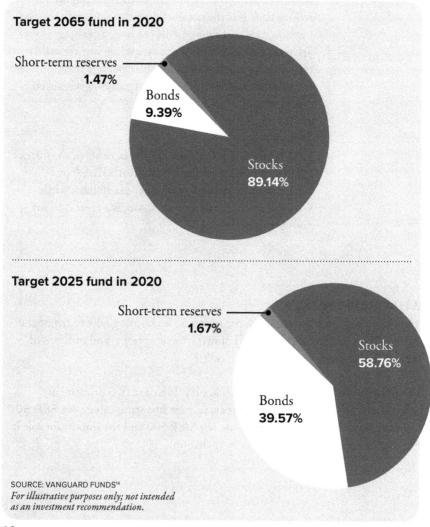

Target 2065 fund in 2020

Short-term reserves
1.47%

Bonds
9.39%

Stocks
89.14%

Target 2025 fund in 2020

Short-term reserves
1.67%

Stocks
58.76%

Bonds
39.57%

SOURCE: VANGUARD FUNDS[14]
For illustrative purposes only; not intended as an investment recommendation.

CHAPTER 8
THE STOCK MARKET AND THE S&P 500

WHAT IS THE S&P 500?

a) 500 of the largest publicly traded companies in the U.S.

b) A supersonic stealth drone

c) A NASCAR race

d) A newly discovered comet circling Neptune

The correct answer is *a)*.

Be honest; would you have answered correctly if this question was on page one? I have asked, *"What is the S&P 500?,"* in hundreds of high school and college classrooms. Are you surprised to learn that often no one knows the answer? Even when pressed? Let's change that.

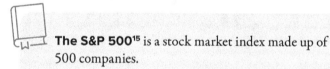

The S&P 500[15] is a stock market index made up of 500 companies.

The companies in the S&P 500 are **based in the United States.**

But they make over **40% of their money selling products and services internationally.**[16]

They **employ more than 20 million people**[17] directly, and millions more indirectly.

They also **support countless small businesses** that sell goods and services to these bigger companies.

These 500 companies are selected as part of a **rigorous process for inclusion** in this widely followed stock-market 'index' that we call *the S&P 500,* or sometimes just *the S&P.*

With over five million employer businesses in the United States,[18] **fewer than 0.009% receive the invitation.**

Importantly, the companies that make up the S&P 500 weren't given or handed their success. **They earned it.**

Companies such as **Amazon and Apple,** which began with an idea in a garage.

Companies that survived the "start-up" period—when close to 90% of businesses fail.[19]

Companies such as **Disney,** that grew slowly and steadily over time.

Others such as **Netflix and Twitter,** that grew far more quickly.

Companies such as **Etsy, Teradyne, and Catalent,** newer members.[20]

Companies such as **Wal-mart,** a dividend aristocrat, that have been in for much longer.

The invitation for a company to be a part of the S&P 500 is not a lifetime guarantee. Once a company gets in, it must work hard to stay in. Companies are added or removed based on how fast they are growing, shrinking, and a multitude of other factors.

The Stock Market

Like any market, the stock market is a joining of buyers and sellers. In this case, the stocks of companies are bought and sold. Stock represents units of ownership in the company that issued (created) it—in order to raise money for operating and growing its business. Stock comes with a claim to share the company's profits, but no right to compensation or liability if the company fails. Your risk is limited to the money you invest.

Microsoft is in the S&P. Bill Gates, the company's founder, famously did not take a single vacation day in his 20's. Isn't that the work ethic you'd like to have helping to make you money?

Do you brush and floss your teeth? A company called **Colgate** makes and sells toothpaste, toothbrushes, and floss. Colgate is in the S&P 500.

Do you buy those items at **Target?** Target is in the S&P 500.

This is a completely different way to think about investing. And publicly traded companies (those with stock traded in the stock market) are legally obligated to operate in the best interests of their shareholders, the people and organizations that own their stock. Do you want to be an owner of these companies? When your friends buy toothpaste, wouldn't it be cool to give them a fist bump, and say, *"Thanks, I own that company."*

Note: The relative gain from investing long-term applies to buying an S&P 500 fund, not individual stocks, which are not the emphasis of this book. Why not individual stocks? Because any company can have an alligator hiding in the closet, *and alligators are scary!* This analogy simply implies that something unexpected can happen to any one company, something that could affect the share price profoundly.

If you do want to buy individual stocks, consider purchasing them in smaller amounts, like adding a leaf (or two) to your tree. Owning individual stocks can be fun and educational. It can give you insight into how a company runs and operates. And if that stock sinks like a stone, a possibility, it won't hurt your longer-term saving and investing goals.

CHAPTER 9
RULES OF INVESTING

The original *Missing Semester* book gave a single Cardinal Rule for financial success.

Let your saving dictate your spending.

It remains *the* most important money rule.

When it comes to broad stock market *investing,* there are **three rules.** They are investing principles intended to guide you toward a financially comfortable future.

1. UNDER-PROMISE AND OVER-DELIVER

Plan for the stock market to under-perform your expectations. And be pleasantly surprised if it doesn't. For example, even though the historical return of the S&P 500 has been 10% a year when averaged over the long term, plan for a long-term average return of 6% a year. Invest the dollar amount necessary to reach your goals using the assumed 6% rate. And if your financial plan calls for saving 25 cents a day, try for 50 cents, just to be safe. If it calls for $3 per day, shoot for $5.

2. BUY A LITTLE BIT, A LOT OF TIMES

The financial industry has a fancy term for this rule. It's called "dollar-cost averaging." The pros do it, and you should, too. Invest a little bit of money each paycheck, or from your bank account daily, weekly, monthly, and stick with that routine.

Doing a little bit, a lot of times, is a great way to invest. This table shows the "what if" effect of having saved just $1 per day, every day of one's career.[21] A "career" here means a work life of 42 years. Don't get lost in the detail; simply scroll down the *S&P 500 Annualized Return* column to see the average annual return for each career period.

Dollar-cost Averaging

Investing one dollar every day is *dollar-cost averaging*. No one knows with any degree of accuracy what the stock market will do tomorrow, next week, next month or next year. Crystal balls from even the best in the investment industry are cloudy in the short term. Long-term, as the table to the right shows, investment forecasts tend to be more accurate.

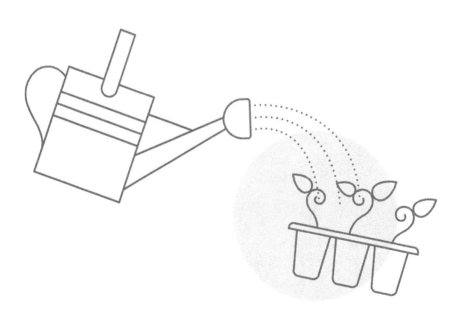

CAREER PERIOD	TOTAL INVESTED	S&P 500 ANNUALIZED RETURN	FINAL VALUE FROM DAILY INVESTMENTS
1978-2019	$15,330	11.84%	$313,690
1977-2018	$15,330	10.91%	$266,487
1976-2017	$15,330	11.60%	$314,963
1975-2016	$15,330	11.91%	$299,418
1974-2015	$15,330	10.80%	$294,163
1973-2014	$15,330	10.35%	$312,602
1972-2013	$15,330	10.47%	$298,464
1971-2012	$15,330	10.08%	$245,688
1970-2011	$15,330	9.79%	$229,914
1969-2010	$15,330	9.51%	$241,357
1968-2009	$15,330	9.42%	$225,385
1967-2008	$15,330	9.36%	$193,531
1966-2007	$15,330	10.30%	$329,198
1965-2006	$15,330	10.46%	$335,548
1964-2005	$15,330	10.48%	$313,414
1963-2004	$15,330	10.89%	$326,460
1962-2003	$15,330	10.38%	$317,175
1961-2002	$15,330	10.34%	$268,911
1960-2001	$15,330	11.01%	$374,231
AVERAGE	$15,330	10.52%	$289,505

3. WHEN SOMETHING OF VALUE THAT YOU WANT TO OWN GOES ON SALE, BUY MORE

When the S&P 500 goes "on sale," *buy more*. In 2008 the stock market dropped 38%.[22] That doesn't happen often. Be ready when it does.

After the drop, charts and pictures make this "buy-low" choice seem easy. It's the opposite of easy. Fear accompanies recessions and stock-market plunges. People you know may lose their jobs, industries may change, companies may close. But we will make it through, and the years will pass. People cited in the news create graphs, point back to the stock-market bottom, and say, *"You should have bought here."* Yes, you should have. Buying more— investing more money—during economic and stock-market slumps is one of the smartest, but most difficult, money choices you can make. Recognize that it is easier recommended than done.

While the value of the stock market (and the S&P 500 stocks as a whole) increases in more years than it decreases, it's important to know that there will be years when your investment account decreases in value. (Next chapter.)

Finally, remember that as you follow the Cardinal Rule—your savings dictating your spending—the decisions that put money in your bank account, for subsequent investment, will remain your best decisions. Then the three rules of investing should help you grow that money wisely.

CHAPTER 10
PREPARING FOR THE WORST

"The two most powerful warriors are patience and time."

—LEO TOLSTOY

Some days it rains a little. Other days it rains a lot. And sometimes it feels like it might never stop raining. Or maybe it's been sunny every day. Grass is turning brown, and it hasn't rained in what feels like ages.

There will be times when investing will feel a lot like this.

Rain is necessary to make things grow; it helps to create beautiful, and essential, things. And a sunny day is hard to beat, but too many rainy or sunny days in a row can have undesirable consequences, as members of the Watching-Trees-Grow Club know.

Keep this in mind the first time you check your investment account only to find you have less money than you had during the previous period. ("My investment account is shrinking!") Yes, you will experience a stock market decline. Yes, you will experience more than one. Here, for perspective, are the ten worst calendar-year declines in returns from the S&P 500 (1926-2019).[23]

WORST CALENDAR-YEAR STOCK MARKET DECLINES

1931	-43.34%
2008	-37.00%
1937	-35.03%
1974	-26.47%
1930	-24.90%
2002	-22.10%
1973	-14.66%
2001	-11.89%
1941	-11.59%
1957	-10.78%

An occasional stock-market decline, even a significant market 'correction,' is not all you face. Throughout modern history there have been recessions and depressions. These are periods, sometimes lasting years, during which economic activity in the nation, or the world, has slowed, jobs are hard to find, and maybe even hard to keep. The amount of money that we (you, I, and every other consumer) are spending is dropping; so companies are going to have a difficult time selling products and services. If companies are selling less, they are likely making less money.

It's like a corporate or economic version of the flu; it takes time for the sick to get better.

Remember the 42-year career periods from Chapter 9? *All* of those periods had at least one recession.

WORST DEPRESSIONS/RECESSIONS
past 100 years[24]

DEPRESSION/RECESSION	STOCK MARKET DECLINE
Great Depression, 1929-1933	-86%
Oil crisis, 1973-1975	-48%
Dotcom bubble, 2001	-49%
Financial crisis, 2007-2009	-57%
Covid-19, 2020*	-34%

*on-going at time of writing

Recession is a scary, but ordinary word. Economic recessions occur more often than you might think. Over the past thirty years, there has been a recession somewhere in the world every two years.[25] Big recessions can be transformative and define the experiences of a generation. Events such as the Covid-19 pandemic, the global financial crisis of 2007-2009, the 9/11 terrorist attacks, and other catastrophic events have lasting effects.

Continuing to invest through stock market corrections and economic recessions takes courage, knowledge, and readiness. When in the moment, we don't and won't know when prices reach bottom. Only hindsight allows us to make charts and tables and circle the numbers at the bottoms. Make your plan (now) to capture this opportunity when it presents itself.

If we knew *when* stock market declines or recessions were going to occur, we could and would do things differently. Unfortunately, that's not how investing, or life, works. Although we don't know what will spark the next correction, recession, depression, it helps to know that you are likely to experience more than one of these. The longer you invest in the stock market the more likely you are to meet your expectations. And if you begin to feel discouraged, remember this.

Betting on the world ending has yet to prove profitable.

CHAPTER 11
THE DIVIDEND REWARD

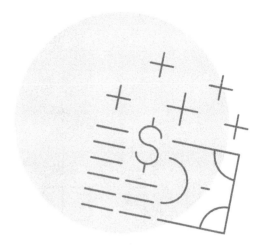

Dividends are like a cash reward for investing.

No joke. You get paid to invest. A dividend is profit that a company shares with its investors-gives back to them- in the form of actual dollars. Over recent history the dividend yield of the S&P 500 has averaged almost 2% a year.[26] This means that for every $100 you invested in the S&P, you were paid back roughly $2 each year in the form of a dividend, your cash reward. For every $1,000 you invested, you were paid back roughly $20. The dividend cash is paid out periodically during the year, not all at once.

Some companies pay out more than 2%, some less, and others don't pay a dividend. This 2% number is the average percent payout of the entire S&P 500, the sum of the dividends paid by all the companies in the index.

Each company determines if and when it pays dividends, and how much it pays.

COMPANIES IN THE S&P 500 WITH THE HIGHEST DIVIDEND YIELD

as of September 2020[27]

COMPANY	DIVIDEND YIELD
Oneok, Inc	14.10%
CenturyLink, Inc.	9.21%
Exxon Mobil Corporation	9.17%
Iron Mountain Incorporated	8.23%
Valero Energy Corporation	8.21%
Kinder Morgan, Inc.	7.94%
Altria Group, Inc.	7.86%
The Williams Companies, Inc.	7.61%
Simon Property Group, Inc.	7.55%
SL Green Realty Corp.	7.48%
S&P 500	**1.80%**

Seeing dividend yields like these raises an obvious question. **Why doesn't every company do this (pay really high dividends)?**

It's a great question.

When a company pays a dividend, it is choosing not to reinvest that money in the future growth of the company. For company management this is a delicate balancing act between giving investors a short-term reward (a dividend) or the possibility of a long-term return (future growth). Most investors want both.

As an investor, you have a choice to make when you receive a dividend. Take the cash (and do whatever you want) or reinvest it (and let it try to earn even more money).

This isn't a topic we need to spend much time on, because there is a simple, but important dividend rule of thumb—particularly when we are speaking about the S&P 500 and the combined dividend yield of those companies.

The dividend rule

Before retirement, reinvest dividends; after retirement, use the money to live.

Ellen, a 20-year old student, is inspired to begin investing. She follows the Cardinal Rule from the first *Missing Semester:* **let saving dictate spending.** She plans to save diligently $3 a day in her Roth IRA for her entire working career. She also participates in her company 401(k), to receive the company match, of course. She views her Roth IRA as a stable source of investment income later in her life, after she quits working, and plans to use her 401(k) money for daily needs and wants in retirement.

She also follows the *dividend rule* and will reinvest her dividends until she is 70. Expecting to live to 100, she has budgeted for 30 years of skydiving, cliff jumping, and various other travel adventures in retirement. Let's look only at the Roth IRA part of her savings. Consider it the "fun fund" because Ellen is going to rely on her 401(k) to cover her basic living expenses in retirement.

EFFECT OF DIVIDENDS, ROTH IRA

AGE	ROTH IRA BEGINNING VALUE	DIVIDENDS PAID	REINVEST DIVIDENDS YES/NO	RETURN ON IRA INVESTMENT	ROTH IRA ENDING VALUE
20-24	$5,590	$134	yes	10%	$7,354
25-29	$16,356	$349	yes	10%	$19,197
30-34	$33,696	$696	yes	10%	$38,270
35-39	$61,621	$1,254	yes	10%	$68,988
40-44	$106,595	$2,154	yes	10%	$118,459
45-49	$179,026	$3,602	yes	10%	$198,133
50-54	$295,677	$5,935	yes	10%	$326,449
55-59	$483,544	$9,693	yes	10%	$533,103
60-64	$786,106	$15,744	yes	10%	$865,921
65-69	$1,273,385	$25,490	yes	10%	$1,401,928
70-74	$1,907,307	$38,146	no	8%	$2,059,892
75-79	$2,802,460	$56,049	no	8%	$3,026,657
80-84	$4,117,733	$82,355	no	8%	$4,447,152
85-89	$6,050,301	$121,006	no	8%	$6,534,326
90-94	$8,889,878	$177,798	no	8%	$9,601,068
95-99	$13,062,147	$261,243	no	8%	$14,107,119

This table assumes that over the course of her career Ellen earns the historical annualized return from the S&P 500 of about 10%.[28] She stuck with it during the hard times. Her assumed return during retirement is 8% because she will begin taking the 2% dividend return as cash after age 70 rather than re-investing it. The point is, when you make a choice to *receive* rather than *reinvest* dividends, you must lower the long-term return assumptions for the stock market by that 2% dividend yield.

At age 70, as she will no longer be working, Ellen will stop saving the $3 per day that had been going into her Roth IRA. Because she also contributed regularly to her 401(k) and can live on those proceeds, Ellen is able to leave her Roth IRA invested in the stock market. But each year she will receive that "cash reward" for investing, the dividend payment.

Adding Ellen's 401(k) plan results to the table would show even more dramatically how attainable financial independence is. That's an exciting *opportunity* each of you has.

Note: If the Roth IRA is Ellen's (or your) only source of income in retirement, a modification of the plan might be wise. Imagine a recession like the 2008 one happening the year she or you turn 70. Having reviewed the situation well before retirement, she (or you) might have decided to invest in a target-date fund, and maybe consulted an experienced financial planner. But right now, contribute to both a Roth IRA and a 401(k), **start young,** and stick with it.

Good execution in the first half of your career will have you well positioned for a strong second half.

CHAPTER 12
WHEN NOT TO INVEST

Here's a question from a recent college graduate. It's a question that comes up frequently and deserves attention.

"Instead of initially investing in my 401(k) and a Roth IRA, I have been thinking about paying off my student loans. I know I would be missing out on the free money I would gain from my 401(k) match, but I'm thinking that wouldn't really matter considering my approximately $47,000 in student loan debt is accruing interest [costing me] daily, and I would like to pay that off as soon as possible.

What do you think about attacking the student loan debt head on and paying that off earlier than expected with additional money that would've gone into a 401(k) and a Roth IRA?"

What do you think? Should this student

a) Pay off student loans and not invest

b) Pay off student loans and invest

c) Not pay off student loans and only invest

Student loans are a legal obligation, which eliminates *c)*. The best answer is *b)*, if you are able. Why? The answer is in the math.

Recall the table in Chapter 6 showing what your career-long investments might add up to. That used the average 4.7%[29] "company match" for a 401(k) plan account, paired with a salary of $50,000. Making a year's 401(k) contribution of $2,350 qualifies you for a match of $2,350 by your employer. Now look at what happens long term if the student asking the above question chooses to participate in that same company 401(k) plan now, at age 22, rather than focusing entirely on paying off student-loan debt and waiting until age 32 to start the 401(k) contributions. To make the high possible cost of delay dramatically clear, the table again assumes the long-term 10% annualized return from the S&P 500.[30]

THE HIGH COST OF DELAY	HYPOTHETICAL 401(K) ACCOUNT VALUE AT AGE 70
Start contributions to 401(k) at 22 years old	$4,900,160
Start contributions to 401(k) at 32 years old	$1,841,958
OPPORTUNITY COST OF WAITING	$3,058,202

A possible $3 million difference in your 401(k) retirement/investment account makes this a question to take seriously. Student loans should not be a deterrent from starting a Roth IRA or participating in a 401(k) plan and receiving the 401(k)-match mentioned. This isn't an either/or decision. Pick up a second job or pick up those overtime hours. In any case, do *not* miss out!

BUT WHEN SHOULD YOU NOT INVEST?

There are still times when you should not invest in the stock market—when other goals take priority, and they deserve attention.

YOU HAVE OUTSTANDING CREDIT CARD DEBT

This is the amount of your credit card bill that you are NOT able to pay in full each month. The median credit card interest rate in the United States is 19.49%.[31] The 'investment return' on credit card debt in this case is -19.49% every year that you don't pay off that balance. This is an anchor holding you back from financial freedom. Eliminating outstanding credit card debt must be the primary goal if you are in this situation.

YOU HAVE SHORT-TERM FINANCIAL NEEDS

The stock market is unpredictable in the short-term. You cannot count on positive investment returns from stocks in the short term, even from an S&P 500 fund. Review the **investing odds** table (opposite page) and set your goals accordingly. Money being set aside for a home, a car, or to meet another short-term financial goal should be put in one of the other money and investment vehicles listed in Chapter 6.

YOU REQUIRE GOVERNMENT AID

Close to 20% of the U.S. population rely on government assistance programs each month.[32] Some of this assistance is affected by or even contingent upon *not* having individual savings and investing accounts.

S&P 500 INVESTING ODDS
1926-2019[33]

INVESTMENT DURATION	ODDS OF MAKING MONEY	ODDS OF LOSING MONEY
1 day	52%	48%
1 week	56%	44%
1 month	59%	41%
1 year	73%	27%
3 years	83%	17%
5 years	87%	13%
10 years	95%	5%
15 years	100%	0%

Author's note to elected and appointed government officials and corporate leaders reading this book
I have received emails from students who wanted to take ownership of their financial future, who wanted to act and take small steps towards having financial freedom. But they learned that if they did so, they would lose critical help being provided by the government. Critical is the correct word. Help shouldn't hold people back. Let's please have this conversation. There are steps we can take today to create financial freedom for everyone, but we can't do it without your help and leadership.

AND WHEN SHOULD YOU TAKE LESS RISK WITH YOUR INVESTMENTS?

WHEN YOU NEAR RETIREMENT
Then it's time to begin rethinking your investment strategy and to re-evaluate your risk tolerance. For example, when will you need this money? How financially comfortable would you be if the stock market declined just as you retired? Moving from riskier investments (stocks) into CDs, bonds, annuities, etc., makes sense at this point if you are counting on this money for daily expenses.

CHAPTER 13
PUTTING IT ALL TOGETHER

So, where do you actually start? Whether you are a student or are starting your first job, let's look at the first few, actual, investment decisions you can or will make.

STUDENT

If you are a high school or college student, *start with a Roth IRA*. Remember from Chapter 4 that neither what your investments earn in the account nor what you take out of the account later in life are taxed. That makes for a huge advantage. Although your contributions to a Roth IRA are made with after-tax earnings, your tax rate is likely to be lower now (see the income-tax rates table, opposite page). So your contributions to a tax-sheltered Roth account (where your investment earnings and gains are free from tax) are relatively inexpensive compared to later in your life.

Your income and its tax rate are likely to increase with your age

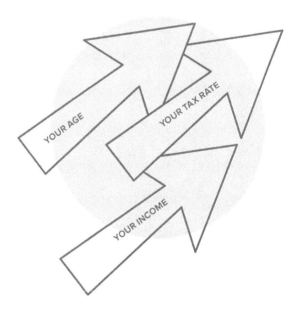

YOUR AGE

YOUR TAX RATE

YOUR INCOME

AGE	AVERAGE TAX RATE
15	2.2%
20	7.1%
25	11.6%
30	13.7%
35	15.2%
40	16.0%
45	17.2%
50	17.6%
55	17.6%
60	17.1%
65	16.1%
70	13.6%
75	11.9%
80	12.3%
85	12.3%
90	11.2%
AVERAGE	15.2%

Later in life your taxes are likely to be higher, much higher—but your withdrawals then come *tax free*.

INCOME-TAX RATES

As the table to the left shows,[34] over time, the tax rate for most people has increased with their age. So to repeat: while you are young, it is inexpensive, in terms of taxes, to put money into your Roth IRA. And the money in the account—as well as the money you take out—is *all yours*.

Another reason a Roth IRA is a big deal: it eliminates a major uncertainty. Specifically, the uncertainty of not knowing what your tax rate will be in the future, when tax rates could be way higher. Less uncertainty means more accuracy in achieving financial goals, making your decisions easier and more likely to pay off.

It's a smart money decision to open a Roth IRA, and to contribute as much as you can, for at least your entire 20s. If you have earned income (that is, from a job), no age is too young to start.

FIRST FULL-TIME JOB

Congratulations! You did it! When starting your first full-time job, take the same smart-money approach as for your student years: open (if you haven't already done this) a Roth IRA and contribute as much as you can throughout your 20s. This step comes with a "but." You have an immediate choice to make with your company 401(k) or retirement plan.

If your company offers a match, TAKE IT. Contribute the minimum amount required to receive the maximum match. For example, if your company matches up to 3% of your salary, contribute 3% of your salary. If the match is 5%, even better. Contribute 5%.

Some employers require you to "opt in" to the 401(k), whereas others automatically enroll you, and you are required to "opt out" if you don't want to invest. *Don't ever opt out.* You'd never opt out of a pension plan (in fact, you can't). This is your personal pension/investment plan. You will be a participant in the company 401(k) plan, an investment account in which you oversee the investments. So give priority to an employer's 401(k) with a matching contribution—because of the match. But also contribute to a Roth IRA, if at all possible. Better yet, ask your company if they offer a **Roth 401(k)** and get the best of both worlds—a company match and the tax benefits of your age.

SWITCHING JOBS

You've done everything right with your saving and investing. You have also worked hard and built your knowledge and skills on the job in this early part of your career. An exciting opportunity has presented itself and you are considering leaving your current company for a new job.

If you take the *new* job, what should you do with your *old* 401(k)? You know not to cash out and spend the money, but when you switch jobs, where does your 401(k) go?

First, the money you invested in the 401(k) is **your money.** It's yours to take with you. The money the company matched is also your money—*if it has "vested,"* an important *if.*

 Vesting is the length of time you must work for the company in order for its match to become your money.

While companies typically begin contributing *the match* on day one, in some cases the money isn't technically yours until you have worked a certain amount of time, at which point it vests, and becomes yours. In some cases vesting occurs immediately; in others, after one year, or several years.

Read your benefits package and ask Human Resources what the vesting period is. It differs by company, and you don't want to lose out on money because you didn't understand your company's vesting schedule.

When you move jobs early in your career, choose between

1. bringing your 401(k) with you to the new job, new company.

2. moving the money into a traditional IRA.

Most (but not all) employers will allow you to transfer your old 401(k) into their company plan. This is called a *401(k) rollover.* If this transfer is not available, you can always transfer the funds to a traditional IRA. No matter what you choose to do, **do not elect to withdraw the funds. Ever. The opportunity cost of doing so is simply too high.**

INVESTING YOUR MONEY

When you build a house, you start with a single brick, stone, or block and build the foundation, *one brick, stone, or block at a time.* Investing works the same way. In the early part of your career, don't over-think things. A strong foundation enables a house to stand up to heavy winds, storms and worse. At this point in your investing life, you are building the foundation for the rest of your life, *one dollar at a time,* with a low-cost S&P index fund or a target-date fund. It really is this simple.

THE SECOND HALF OF LIFE

As you grow your wealth, your assets, and your family, your financial decisions are likely to become more complicated. Good, professional financial advisors can be helpful in assessing the big picture and helping you construct a plan to make your money last, so that you can enjoy spending it and/or giving it to others. But with all you will have learned by then about investing, you may be able to navigate your own way. Your choice.

People who are able to give money to charity frequently report that giving their money away is more pleasurable and satisfying than earning it or having it.

It's fun giving money to causes you care about.

Especially when you can afford to do so.

THE BOTTOM LINE
WHY MONEY MATTERS

"It's not about what it is. It's about what it can become."

—DR. SEUSS

What almost no retiree says: "I have too much money."

What most retirees do say: "I wish I had started saving earlier."

Why? Because money allows us to spend time with people we love, in places we love, doing the things we love to do. This is financial independence. This is the goal of the *Missing Semester* series. The irony in what The *Missing Second Semester* is trying to teach is that as we age, money and material items decline in value and **time** (the thing that we have so much of when we are young) increases in value.

Before reading this book, did you look at interest as something you could earn? Or count the opportunity cost of major expenses? Did you think of investing as having millions of people working to help you to achieve your financial goals? Of not just buying toothpaste, but buying a piece of the company that makes and sells that toothpaste?

The investment concepts here are time tested and proven *if you stick with them.* Because of the retirement changes that we have mentioned, knowing about investing isn't important, it's imperative!

There has never been more need for our Watching-Trees-Grow Club. *Everyone* is invited to join. That tree outside your school window? Someone *just like you,* planted it. And it worked!

The Cardinal Rule from the previous *Missing Semester* will always be the most important.

Save first.

It really is that simple.

The Missing Second Semester is to help you grow the money you save—to give you the courage and the understanding for **financial empowerment.** When we are young, we should be more afraid of *not* investing, than of choosing to invest.

1. Start today

2. Stick with it

3. Don't quit

The world is at your fingertips. Avoid money mistakes, and it always will be.

Your age is an extraordinary opportunity. Powerful enough to change your life.

Now go do it. You're in charge.

Author's note
Since writing the first *Missing Semester,* I have had the privilege, the honor, and the pleasure of speaking in hundreds of high school and college classrooms across the country. No matter where I've been, no matter the zip code or the classroom demographics, the questions are the same. And the hope is unmistakable. It's clear you can do it. Our collective future is in good hands, because it's in your hands. I believe that.

ACKNOWLEDGEMENTS

The Missing Second Semester *would not have been possible without the help of a committed and talented team. To the many reviewers, readers, friends and to the Troutwood team who dedicated time to this effort, thank you for your honest and thoughtful feedback.*

Stewart Smith, we did it again! It is an absolute joy working with you, and this book is better because of your efforts and persistence. Phoebe Smith and Hunt Smith Design, thank you for your hard work and creativity on the interior design and layout. Brian Taylor, thank you for your thoughtfulness and vision in designing the book cover. Matt Kabala and Jeff Davidek, you might as well be family, and I appreciate your constant voices throughout this undertaking.

And because it is rare in life to have this opportunity, to my wife Whitney—I love you, I love our family, and I love sharing the journey that our life is with you beside me. Thank you for your patience and your support.

With sincere appreciation and gratitude to all,

Gene

SOURCES

CHAPTER 1

1. Federal Reserve Bank of New York
    newyorkfed.org/microeconomics/hhdc.html

CHAPTER 3

2. Health insurance
    healthcare.gov/young-adults/children-under-26/

3. Roth IRA early withdrawal
    irs.gov/taxtopics/tc557

CHAPTER 4

4. Historical return of S&P 500, Investopedia
    investopedia.com/ask/answers/042415/what-average-annual-return-sp-500.asp

5. Opportunity-cost calculation, Bankrate
    bankrate.com/calculators/savings/compound-savings-calculator-tool.aspx

CHAPTER 5

6. Historical return of S&P 500, Investopedia
    investopedia.com/ask/answers/042415/what-average-annual-return-sp-500.asp

7. Opportunity-cost calculation, Bankrate
    bankrate.com/calculators/savings/compound-savings-calculator-tool.aspx

CHAPTER 6

8. 45% of Americans don't invest, Gallup
    news.gallup.com/poll/1711/stock-market.aspx

9. Average company match (2019)
    Fidelity Q1 2019 Retirement Trends

10. Average U.S. salary (2018)
    ssa.gov/oact/cola/central.html

11. FDIC insurance coverage
    fdic.gov/deposit/covered/notinsured.html

CHAPTER 7

12. 401(k)
    irs.gov/retirement-plans/401k-resource-guide

13. Roth IRA
    irs.gov/retirement-plans/roth-iras

14. Vanguard target-date funds
    a. *investor.vanguard.com/mutual-funds/profile/portfolio/vlxvx*
    b. *investor.vanguard.com/mutual-funds/profile/portfolio/vttvx*

CHAPTER 8

15. Companies in the S&P 500
    slickcharts.com/sp500

16. S&P statistics: revenue
    us.spindices.com/indexology/djia-and-sp-500/sp-500-global-sales

17. S&P statistics: number of employees
    investors.com/etfs-and-funds/sectors/sp500-the-u-s-top-employers-are-holding-up-in-coronavirus-crash/

18. Number of employer companies in the United States
    cdn.advocacy.sba.gov/wp-content/uploads/2019/04/23142719/2019-Small-Business-Profiles-US.pdf

19. Start-up failure rate
    national.biz/2019-small-business-failure-rate-startup-statistics-industry/

20. Newest S&P 500 companies
    cnn.com/2020/09/04/investing/tesla-sp-500-etsy/index.html

CHAPTER 9

21. Historical S&P 500 returns
    slickcharts.com/sp500/returns

22. S&P 500, 2008 calendar-year return
    slickcharts.com/sp500/returns

CHAPTER 10

23. S&P 500 ten worst calendar years
    slickcharts.com/sp500/returns

24. Recession data: JP Morgan Guide to Markets, 3Q 2020

25. IMF recession number
    imf.org/en/Publications/WP/Issues/2018/03/05/How-Well-Do-Economists-Forecast-Recessions-45672

CHAPTER 11

26. Historical dividend yield of S&P
    ycharts.com/indicators/sp_500_dividend_yield

27. Top-ten Dividend Ranking
    S&P Capital IQ

28. Historical S&P return
    investopedia.com/ask/answers/042415/what-average-annual-return-sp-500.asp

CHAPTER 12

29. Average company match
Fidelity Q1 2019 Retirement Trends

30. Historical S&P data
investopedia.com/ask/answers/042415/what-average-annual-return-sp-500.asp

31. Median credit-card interest rate, Investopedia
investopedia.com/average-credit-card-interest-rate-5076674

32. U.S. government assistance, Urban Institute
urban.org/sites/default/files/publication/99674/five_things_you_may_not_know_about_the_us_social_safety_net_1.pdf

33. S&P 500 investing odds
slickcharts.com/sp500/returns

CHAPTER 13

34. Tax rate
users.nber.org/~taxsim/byage/

NOTES

CPSIA information can be obtained
at www.ICGtesting.com
Printed in the USA
LVHW041302240223
740095LV00007B/16